KEEP IT LEGAL

The Law for Radio, Podcasting
and Social Media

by Paul Chantler
and
Paul Hollins

Liability Disclaimer

This book is not a substitute for seeking personalised professional legal advice. It should be understood that the pages of this book do not purport to offer any kind of legal advice whatsoever whether or not implied.

Laws can and do vary widely between countries and jurisdictions; you should therefore always endeavour to do your own thorough due diligence to ensure full compliance with local governing laws.

The author, publisher, distributor and any other third-party associated with this book will not be held responsible under any circumstances for any action taken in whole or in part in respect of the information contained herein.

By reading this book, you assume all risks associated with using the advice given, with a full understanding that you, solely, are responsible for anything that may occur as a result of putting this information into action in any way, and regardless of your interpretation of the advice. Therefore, this book should be considered for use as general entertainment purposes only.

Terms of Use

You are given a non-transferable, "personal use" license to this product. You cannot distribute it or share it with other individuals. It is for your own personal use only.

All copyrights and trademarks remain the sole right of their respective owner. All stories and examples shown are for illustration purposes only.

© 2017 Paul Chantler & Paul Hollins

Contents

Introduction 5
Part 1: Defamation The Right to a Good Name 7
        Appendix: The McAlpine Case 32
Part 2: Contempt of Court The Right to a Fair Trial 39
Part 3: Injunctions The Right to Privacy 51
About the Authors 54

Introduction

The idea of this book is to show you how the law can affect what you say on the radio, in a podcast or when you're blogging or using social media such as Twitter and Facebook.

It's not about scaremongering or making you worry unnecessarily. It's simply about helping reduce the risk of finding yourself at the centre of very expensive legal action.

Both of us have spent lifetimes in the radio industry. Our first book was a legal guide for broadcasters. Then we came up with a second book for a wider readership with advice and information for social media users and bloggers.

Keep It Legal combines and updates the two and we hope it'll be a handy, easy-to-understand guide to a complex area of the law which is becoming increasingly relevant for media on-air, online or on mobile.

Because social media is so important in the daily lives of young people, we strongly believe basic legal knowledge as it relates to Twitter and Facebook should be a subject taught in schools.

Teenagers think they can pull out their phones and write anything they like online – but they need to know just how far they can go. It's only by making the dos and dont's of social media part of teaching in schools that we can be sure the message gets through.

Many radio managers think the biggest danger to their company comes from journalists. The reality is, though, that it is their presenters and DJs who are the biggest threat.

At least journalists usually have some legal training in college and read off pre-prepared scripts. However, many presenters ad lib their links and are untrained in media law.

Keep It Legal

It is no coincidence that the two biggest legal catastrophes in commercial radio in the last 20 years were caused by presenters rather than journalists.

And the next big legal problem in radio will probably be caused by Johnny Jock on Radio Nowhere's breakfast show commenting on allegations he read on Twitter about the local mayor. Very dangerous.

Whether you're on the radio, making a podcast, tweeting on Twitter, posting on Facebook or writing a blog we believe this guide will give you the knowledge to keep on the right side of the law.

We've divided it into three sections – Defamation, Contempt of Court and Injunctions.

Please note that all our content is based on the legal system of England and Wales, although there is a word or two about the differences in Scotland and Northern Ireland. The detail of libel law differs in other jurisdictions, so please be sure to check.

Paul Chantler and Paul Hollins

Part 1
Defamation
The Right to a Good Name

We Have Free Speech in the UK, Don't We?

Well actually, NO.

The concept of free speech in the UK is really a myth. You can only speak or write freely after obeying certain laws.

In the United States, it's different as there is a legal right to free speech under the First Amendment of the US Constitution.

What is Defamation?

The word defamation literally means to "defame" someone. In other words, harming their reputation or good name.

The law says everyone has a right to a good name throughout their lives unless there is undeniable evidence to the contrary such as being convicted of a crime.

Defamation is divided into two parts – LIBEL and SLANDER.

- LIBEL is written defamation in a newspaper, book, magazine, website, social media such as Twitter or Facebook – or broadcast on radio or television as well as in podcasts.
- SLANDER is spoken defamation. Anyone making a claim for slander has to prove actual loss or damage, for example that someone has lost money or their job.

Keep It Legal

Despite broadcast speech being spoken, it's considered to be libel rather than slander because it's effectively 'published' to a large number of people through transmission.

People sometimes also take action for MALICIOUS FALSEHOOD. This means a statement is a lie told with malice. In other words, the person making it knew what they were saying was false and would cause harm or damage.

What is Libel?

Libel is anything published or broadcast which "tends to":

- Expose someone to HATRED, RIDICULE, CONTEMPT or DISGRACE.
- Lead someone to be SHUNNED or AVOIDED.
- Injure someone in their BUSINESS, OFFICE, TRADE or PROFESSION.
- Lower someone in the eyes of "right-thinking members of society generally".

Someone who brings a claim for libel is called a claimant and the person defending it is a defendant.

The use of the phrase "tends to" means claimants don't have to prove any of these things happened. The burden of proof is on you (see later).

What Can Be Defamatory?

All sorts of things can be potentially defamatory ranging from accusing someone of taking a bribe to being a liar, taking illegal drugs, being a paedophile or terrorist, misusing their position for personal gain and committing a crime they didn't do.

Who Can Claim for Libel and What Has to be Proved?

Any living individual can start a legal claim for libel. For a libel action to succeed against you, someone ONLY has to prove the statement you made is:

- Defamatory
- Refers to them
- Published or broadcast by you
- Did serious reputational harm

You can't defame the dead.

In England and Wales, libel actions have to be started within one year of first publication or broadcast.

Businesses, companies and organisations can also start a libel action if they can prove serious financial loss.

The Burden of Proof is on YOU!

Almost uniquely in English law, the burden of proof in libel cases lies with the writer and publisher NOT the claimant.

In other words, YOU have to be able to prove that what you write on your blog or social media page is true. The person you're talking about doesn't have to prove that you're wrong or any statement about them is false.

For example, if you described someone on a radio show, podcast or in a tweet as a "junkie" and they took action against you, it's up to you to prove in court that they are a drug addict.

One of the most effective ways to protect yourself against the threat of libel is to use only verifiable facts. A verifiable fact is one that is capable of being proven true or false.

So, ask yourself - Is this true? Can I prove it? Would I like this said about me?

"Nudge Nudge, Wink Wink…"

Libel is all about the meaning of words or phrases.

It also covers the following:

INNUENDO – something attributed to the words by people who have a specialist knowledge

INFERENCE – reading between the lines without any specialist knowledge

IMPLICATION – something suggested without being directly or explicitly stated

How Does Libel Affect Radio and Podcasts?

When you're on-air or putting out a podcast, you have the power to influence - and that comes with huge responsibility.

As a presenter, it's vitally important that you are aware of your legal obligations because the consequences of getting it wrong can be severe for both you and your radio station.

Although most libel cases are brought against newspapers, it doesn't mean that radio stations, presenters and podcasts are exempt.

A slip of the tongue can result in a claim for libel.

By law, all radio stations have to keep a recorded 'log' of their output for 42 days. This means if a libel comment is broadcast, then the station will have a copy of it. Chances are you will need to provide this recording in court so an overview of context can be considered.

How Does Libel Affect Twitter, Facebook and Blogs?

Although social media may feel like a place for informal discussion, opinions and banter, you are effectively publishing or broadcasting what you say like newspapers and traditional media.

You may feel safe writing a tweet or post on your smart phone in a coffee shop, but when you press the send button you are publishing what you say and the implications can have huge consequences.

Libel law protects individuals and organisations from unwarranted, mistaken or untruthful attacks on their reputation and good name.

When you post on a blog or on Twitter or Facebook, you have a REAL responsibility for what you write.

You may be able to delete your comments from your device - but your words are stored somewhere on a server and, as we shall see, you can be traced and held responsible.

You can end up being sued personally for damages and the legal costs which could run into thousands of pounds.

A lack of knowledge is no defence. Saying it was just a joke is no defence. A casual, throw-away remark can result in legal action against you.

The First 'Twibel' Cases

Courtney Love

US singer Courtney Love paid more than £260,000 ($430,000) in 2011 to settle the world's first Twitter Libel – or 'Twibel' – lawsuit.

She agreed an out-of-court settlement with her fashion designer Dawn Simorangkir rather than risk going to trial over what legal papers described as a string of defamatory comments in tweets on her former Twitter account courtneylover79.

Among other things, Ms Simorangkir was accused of being "a nasty, lying hosebag thief".

Ms Love, the widow of Nirvana frontman Kurt Cobain, argued that her rantings were merely an opinion and that Ms Simorangkir couldn't prove how they damaged her.

But the designer claimed Ms Love was influential as an entertainer and noted the power of social media to disseminate damaging comments.

Even though the case didn't go to trial, it's set a disturbing precedent in the US where freedom of speech generally trumps accusations of libel.

<u>Colin Elsbury</u>

Meanwhile, a former mayor of Caerphilly in South Wales made legal history when he became the first person in Britain to pay damages for libel on Twitter.

Colin Elsbury was ordered by the High Court in Cardiff to pay £3,000 compensation after he mistakenly tweeted that political rival Eddie Talbot had to be removed by police from a polling station.

In addition to the payment of damages, Mr Elsbury was also left with a bill for legal costs of about £50,000.

He also had to publish a formal apology on his Twitter feed for damaging Mr Talbot's reputation and for causing him to suffer anger, upset and ridicule.

If You Can't Prove It – Don't Post It!

One of the most important points is to make absolutely sure that what you write on Twitter, Facebook and your blog is 100% true.

Do NOT make claims or accusations that you cannot prove in court.

Even if you think you can prove it, still be very cautious as proving things in court can be very difficult indeed.

You'll have to use robust documentary evidence or first-hand corroboration from one or more people willing to testify in court.

Therefore, it's essential you make sure you get your facts right before you say what you think of an individual or organisation online.

You Can't Delete Tweets

There is a 'dustbin' or 'trash can' icon underneath every tweet sent - but clicking it does not mean the message is thrown on an electronic rubbish dump.

It stays briefly on Twitter's searchable index of messages and can be found for much longer on mainstream search engines, though finding specific tweets can be difficult.

All messages are preserved on Twitter's computer servers even if they are not publicly viewable.

This means that what you write on Twitter stays on Twitter forever despite your best efforts to delete.

Bloggers Beware!

Bloggers think that free speech allows them to write -and encourage others to write – what they like.

They can't. The law of libel applies to them and their contributors too.

Bloggers have to be particularly careful if they allow comments on their blogs.

Comments can be administered in two ways on blogs – firstly, "We never moderate – all comments go up automatically", and secondly, "All comments are read and manually approved".

The latter approach gives a better quality of comment but can also bring a potential legal danger.

If a comment has been reviewed and published by the blogger and the comment in subsequently found to be libellous, it is the BLOGGER who's responsible and not the original author of the comment.

The blogger has simply repeated a libel.

Beware Anonymous Posts

If a blog or website fails to take down a user's anonymous defamatory post after receiving a complaint, they risk being treated as the primary publisher and sued for libel.

The Defamation Act 2013 says blogs and websites have libel protection if they act quickly to remove anonymous postings which prompt a complaint.

"Allegedly" Won't Protect You

Comedians Paul Merton and Ian Hislop have a lot to answer for when it comes to libel.

Their use of the word "allegedly" over the years on the satirical TV quiz Have I Got News For You became a running joke – and has lulled people into believing that if they used it too, they can say what they like about anyone.

Nothing could be further from the truth.

In fact, using the word allegedly before a potentially dodgy remark about someone gives the clear impression you REALISE what you're about to say is dangerous.

It's perceived as admittance that you're not sure whether what you're saying is true.

Why 'Comedy' is No Defence

Despite the wigs and gowns worn by lawyers and judges in court, the law does NOT have a sense of humour!

Have I Got News For You is the perfect example of why TV and radio comedy shows get away with not being sued for libel.

If things are presented in a light-hearted or satirical way on a comedy show, there's far less chance of being sued than if allegations are on a news bulletin.

The key is that people must be aware of the type of show.

Many TV and radio comedy shows air comments and insults about celebrities and politicians – but it is done within the context of a well-established and well-known format which ordinary viewers and listeners are unlikely to take seriously.

Merton and Hislop have built a reputation for comedy and satire over the years. The show is also cleverly edited to give the impression that 'anything goes' and the participants can say whatever they want.

In reality, the content is screened by a professional team of lawyers ahead of transmission to ensure anything broadcast stays well within acceptable boundaries.

However, a blog, a podcast, a tweet or a radio station breakfast show does not necessarily have a reputation for comedy or satire like Have I Got News For You.

Keep It Legal

On radio, for example, humour sits alongside serious information such as traffic news. The law takes the view, "How could the casual listener know you're making a joke?"

When you're on-air remember that a joke or throw-away comment can easily be libellous.

Even if you make clear a comment you make is a joke, it can still get you into trouble.

A highly-experienced presenter on a UK radio station read out an email from a listener inquiring about someone who used to be on-air on that station some years before.

The presenter named the person and said: "He's alright. He's just come out of prison. The kiddy fiddling charges were dropped." He laughed as he quickly added, "…only joking of course!"

The radio station was sued for libel by the person referred to - and had to pay damages of several thousand pounds and broadcast an apology.

Can Repeating a Libel Get You into Trouble?

YES. Simply repeating a libel is enough for someone to take legal action against you?

In the eyes of the law, it doesn't matter if you're quoting from another source; if you repeat a libel you are as much to blame for publishing it as the original source.

Always be VERY CAREFUL when using a newspaper or magazine story as the basis of a link on your radio show, or a blog or a tweet. Some sites are more trustworthy than others, for example the BBC website. But be careful when using sites like Wikipedia which can be amended by users.

Many people – celebrities in particular - have taken legal action over stories that were found to be untrue.

And be careful about retweeting other people's tweets. If you retweet, you are equally responsible for repeating a potentially defamatory remark.

Always exercise EXTREME CARE when using a newspaper story, social media or a website as a source.

Many radio stations use newspaper or website stories as the basis of celebrity gossip. This could repeat a story that was later found to be libellous. By repeating a libel on-air, your radio station could also be sued as well as the original source.

The breakfast show team at a radio station in the South of England once read an item from a tabloid newspaper in their 'showbiz news' slot, referring to the marital problems of a famous comedian.

The comedian in question lived in the radio station's area, heard the item – and successfully sued both the newspaper and radio station as the information was untrue.

Can Libel Action be Taken If You're Abusive?

NO. There's a distinction between defamatory statements and vulgar abuse. Libel has to be more than just an insult.

For example, you can say: "I hate Bill Bloggs. He's a tosser" as that's just an insult. However, if you were to say: "I hate Bill Bloggs. He's a tosser and a liar", you would have to prove he was a liar in court if he took libel action against you.

Is Honest Opinion Allowed?

YES OF COURSE! The law allows people to have honestly-held opinions.

Keep It Legal

An honestly-held opinion is not libellous in itself as long as the opinion is not malicious, derogatory or could cause harm to someone's reputation.

This means you can express strong and even spiteful views about someone as long as what you say is recognisable as a comment, based on true facts.

This means we can criticise things we see on TV, the stage and in sports without fear of legal action.

You can criticise someone's performance – but to imply they weren't trying could be libellous.

You can't go over-the-top with criticism either.

The actress Charlotte Cornwall sued tabloid newspaper the Sunday People and its columnist Nina Myskow in 1985 for commenting about a theatre performance in her 'Wally of the Week' column: "She can't sing, her bum is too big and she has the sort of stage presence that jams lavatories."

She was awarded £11,000 damages because the judge said that criticism must not "pass out of the domain of criticism itself." In other words, critics can't make derogatory statements in the guise of criticism.

Can You Libel Businesses?

YES. You can libel businesses, companies and organisations as well as individuals.

A radio station in the North West was sued by a couple who ran a caravan holiday business after complaints from customers were aired during a consumer feature.

During an interview on-air, the presenter referred to one of the couple as a "con man". He sued for libel.

During the hearing, the radio station produced 20 unhappy former customers. The company produced 20 customers who were happy. The court had to decide whether the man was habitually dishonest.

In the end, the company won £350,000 damages from the radio station.

If You Don't Name the Person, Does That Make It OK?

NO. Again, this is a popular misconception. The law states that if the person is simply identifiable then they can take legal action.

The word 'identifiable' is key as it means that even if you don't directly name the person, they can still launch legal proceedings against you if people can work out who they are from what you said or the way you described them.

If a person or group can establish that the offending words apply to them, they have a case.

It's difficult for action to be taken in the case of wide generalisations but not as things get more specific.

For example, "All estate agents are liars and cheats" is unlikely to be actionable. But if you say, "All estate agents in Blanktown High Street are liars and cheats", they're identifiable and could all take you to court.

Celebs are Fair Game Though, Right?

WRONG. It's a mistake to think that just because someone chooses to be in the public eye that they're 'fair game' and that you can, therefore, say anything you like about them.

There are numerous examples of libel pay-outs when inaccurate stories about celebrities and their private lives have been splashed over the pages of a newspaper.

Keep It Legal

Actor and singer Jimmy Nail won a libel action against Galaxy Radio in the North East and the Newcastle Chronicle newspaper when they described how "stroppy" he was during filming.

The radio station's breakfast show aired callers telling stories about how "difficult", "demanding" and "tight with money" he was alleged to be. He was awarded £15,000 damages.

No-One Famous Will Ever Know If I Libel Them

WRONG. It's dangerous to think along those lines because even if you work in a very small radio marketplace, streaming and digital media now mean you potentially have a much wider audience, so you never know who might be listening.

These days it's not just your local FM or AM transmission area you're broadcasting to.

Many famous people employ companies to monitor the media to ensure nothing defamatory or derogatory is being said or written about them. And many radio stations have 'listen again' features where broadcast programmes and archived.

It's worth remembering that the person who you've libelled (famous or not) doesn't need to have heard it with their own ears to take action. In fact, they don't even need to have heard it at the time of transmission.

Many celebrities have fans which tweet anything said by the media about them making it easy for the stars themselves or their representatives to find out what's been said.

If they do make a legal complaint you may be required by law to supply a recording from your own 'logger'.

The point is… don't just assume that because you work in a smaller market that you won't be found out.

'Rumours' and 'Wicked Whispers' Are Risky

A comment can still be libellous even if it is reported as a rumour.

Worse still, it can also be libellous even if it is reported as being untrue.

For example, if you were to say something like, "There's a rumour going around that Frank at the corner-shop has been selling out-of-date food, but don't worry because the stuff I've bought there has always been fine" it could still be considered libellous.

This is because the 'rumour part' is based on a defamatory comment which you are effectively repeating.

Therefore if 'Frank' believes that because you mentioned this rumour exists that you are perpetuating it, he could claim that you are further damaging his name, reputation and trade; and as a result, could take action against you.

If he were to do so, remember he is under no obligation to prove that he HASN'T been selling out-of-date food, but you may have to prove in court that he was because you repeated the libellous rumour.

Always take great care with how you approach rumours, so you don't put yourself at risk.

Take Care with Callers & Guests

On radio, if you take callers live to air or have guests in the studio or down the line, remember that something THEY say could be libellous too.

In a live situation, you're partially protected from being sued for libel by what's called the Live Defence – otherwise known legally as Innocent Dissemination.

Keep It Legal

This defence says that there's a legal protection if the following factors apply:

- You were live on-air
- Took all reasonable precautions to ensure a libel didn't happen
- You no reason to suspect it would happen
- You had no effective control over the speaker

Remember, though, it applies only to the guest or caller – not you or any other radio professional who are deemed to know better.

If you suspect a libel is happening live, you should immediately stop your guest or caller (so they don't repeat the libel), offer an apology without repeating it yourself and make sure you distance the radio station from the comments.

This won't mean you 'get off' with the libel, but it will show the courts that you took swift and decisive action.

Always be on your guard and keep your wits about you, even in the most innocent of circumstances.

A presenter at a station in the South East of England was talking to an eight-year-old competition contestant on the phone. During the chat, the presenter asked about the child's school, his favourite subjects and favourite teacher. He also asked, "Who's the worst teacher in the school?"

It was obviously meant as a bit of fun – but by asking this question, the youngster named the teacher whose reputation suffered as a result.

The teacher – financially backed by her union – threatened to sue the station. An out-of-court settlement was reached.

Beware "Creative" Radio Promos

On radio, it's not just live links that are legally risky. Pre-recorded promos and trails can also be potentially libellous.

The former managing director of a radio station in the South of England threatened to take defamation action against the new owners over the content of a promo.

During the MD's time at the station, budgets were tight and the station ran competitions with a joke cash prize of one pound and a penny to match the station's 101 FM frequency.

The new owners touted their big money cash contest with a promo in which an American voiceover said: "Do you remember when the boss of this station ran a competition which gave away a pound and a penny? Well we've just sacked the guy! And now we're giving away £10,000…" The promo had aired more than 20 times.

The MD had left by mutual agreement and had not been sacked. He argued he was clearly identifiable as, though not named, he had been the only boss of the station up till that time.

He threatened to take libel action against the new owners for "damaging him in his trade, office or profession" (see earlier libel definition) unless they stopped the promo being aired, apologised and paid damages. The matter was settled out-of-court.

In another case, a high-profile DJ on a station in the North of England threatened to take action against a smaller rival because of a promo it ran when he left. We have changed the names of the station and the DJ.

The promo, which aired multiple times over several weeks, said: "Radio ABC – the station that promised Johnny Jock a job if he ever left Radio XYZ. Well he has. And our floors have never been cleaner. Thanks, Johnny".

The DJ's lawyer argued the promo "lowered him in the eyes of right-thinking members of the public generally" (see earlier libel definition) and requested the station cease and desist playing it while reserving the right to take action for libel and malicious falsehood.

The smaller station said they thought it was humour the DJ would have enjoyed and offered to apologise on-air multiple times. The matter went no further.

Can I Get into Trouble For 'Liking' Facebook Posts?

Generally, NO. But a case in Switzerland in 2017 shows you may have to be careful in the future.

In the first case of its kind, a man who 'liked' Facebooks post accusing another man of anti-Semitism and racism was convicted of defamation.

The posts came about during discussions on Facebook over which animal welfare groups should be allowed to take part in a large vegan street festival.

Posts describing Erwin Kessler, the president of an animal rights group, as racist, anti-Semitic or fascist, were liked by a number of people.

Mr Kessler then brought a case against the 45-year-old unnamed defendant from Zurich, arguing that by liking the posts the man spread their content by making them visible to a larger number of people and that he acted with intent to harm and without any justifiable cause.

Zurich court judge Catherine Gerwig said at the trial that a 'like' is associated with a positive, meaning he clearly supported the posts' content. The court ruled that the defendant couldn't prove that the statements about Mr Kessler were true.

However, media lawyer Martin Steiger says the conviction should not be taken to mean that from now on anyone liking posts may be at risk of being prosecuted for defamation.

Consequences – Costs and Saying Sorry

If you have action taken against you for libel, the legal fees and payment of damages can run into thousands – and sometimes hundreds of thousands - of pounds.

All radio stations have defamation insurance which covers the costs of fees and damages. However, like home or motor insurance, the premium paid rockets if the insurance is subject to a claim so libel can cost a station real cash.

In addition, there will usually be a large excess. This effectively means most stations settle libel claims directly without invoking the insurance so again, it can cost real cash.

It is possible – though unlikely – that someone suing a station for libel might also take action against you as an individual.

As a radio presenter (whether freelance or employed), a podcaster or if you post, tweet or blog regularly, it may be worth considering 'Professional Indemnity Insurance' which covers you in the unfortunate event of a legal case being taken against you.

Choose a reputable insurer and enquire about taking out a policy, especially if you are a breakfast or talk show host.

The other cost to consider, apart from the ones above, is that of personal impact. Being the subject of legal action puts huge pressure on an individual financially, emotionally and professionally.

Bear in mind that if a case were to be brought against you the radio station you currently work for may:

a) Fire you for bringing yourself (and/or them) into disrepute

b) Expect YOU to indemnify THEM against any costs they incur (i.e. you are responsible for any fines/damages levied against the station). Check your contract to see if this is the case (it usually is)

Any libel action also means an increase in paperwork and meetings for your bosses as they try to sort things out with the lawyers and insurers.

In addition to damages and costs, the settlement of a libel action usually requires an apology either read out in court or, from time to time, on-air.

Apologies need careful wording so leave this to the lawyers and don't try to say sorry yourself without advice as it could get you into even more trouble.

Beware – Trade Unions

It costs a lot of money in legal fees to pursue a claim for libel. Of course, celebrities and high-earners can afford this. You might think that the high cost would put off people in ordinary jobs such as police officers, teachers, doctors, nurses and prison staff.

But the legal costs of all these workers are usually underwritten by their trade union or professional organisation as part of their membership meaning they have deep pockets when it comes to claiming for defamation.

An Apology for Tweeting, Malaysian-Style

In Malaysia, a political activist agreed to apologise multiple times on Twitter in an unusual settlement of a libel case.

Fahmi Fadzil agreed he had defamed a magazine called Female and a publishing company, BluInc Media.

As part of the settlement, he retracted what he'd said and sent a tweet apologising 100 times over three days to make amends.

Things You Should Avoid Saying & Doing

Here are some specific things you should avoid saying about people to ensure you don't find yourself in legal trouble.

- Accusing people of crimes they have not committed
- Alleging they are incompetent
- Alleging they are a hypocrite
- Alleging they are obnoxious
- Alleging they are negligent
- Alleging they are dishonest or immoral
- Accusing them of sexual or financial impropriety
- Accusing them of lying
- Accusing them of doing disreputable deeds

Other 'Danger Words'

Here is also a list of 'Danger Words' - words you should be very cautious about using when talking about people as they could all lead to legal action.

This list is by no means exhaustive but it will give you a good idea of the types of words you should always strive to avoid:

Adulterous, bankrupt, bribery, compulsive liar, communist, con, corrupt, coward, criminal, crook, drug addict, drug dealer, evil, fake, fraud, fascist, gold-digger, like Hitler, homosexual, hypocrite, immoral, incompetent, insane, insolvent, junkie, liar, mafia, mentally diseased, misappropriated funds, Nazi, odd-ball, paranoid, pervert, pimp, plagiarist, prostitute, queer, racist, rapist, retarded, rip-off, satanic, scab, shyster, sleazebag, slut, snitch, spy, stupid, swindling, thieving, traitorous, unethical, unprofessional, unscrupulous, unsound, vile.

Keep It Legal

It's A Matter of Context

There are times where you need to exercise a greater level of care when making a comment or describing a person in order to avoid libel.

For example, it's fine to describe someone as 'all fingers and thumbs' in everyday life, however if you were using that adjective to describe a prominent neurosurgeon then it could be deemed libellous.

This is because the description you have used is derogatory.

A neurosurgeon naturally needs a steady hand, so being described as "all fingers and thumbs" leads to a negative perception.

This could easily damage his reputation and therefore cause harm to him/her professionally.

The area of context is one where you, as broadcaster, need to take great care. Even if what you're saying is intended as humour, the impact of your words could see you on the wrong side of law.

Defences to a Libel Action

There are four main defences to libel:

- The Truth – (formerly called Justification). The matter is true both in substance and in fact. Remember, though, the burden of proof is on you. This means you may have to produce evidence in court in the form of witnesses and documents. If the substance is sufficiently true, a court may overlook minor details of fact.
- Honest Opinion – (formerly called Fair Comment) If the remarks are statements of opinion rather than fact, then it's an acceptable defence to say that the comment was made in good faith, without malice and on a matter of public concern.
- Privilege - This is a complex legal defence based on public interest, which applies to parliament, court hearings and public

meetings. Absolute Privilege covers what MPs say in Parliament and what anyone says in court. Qualified Privilege protects accurate and fair reports of those proceedings which is why broadcasters, newspapers and websites can say what was said without action being taken against them.
- Live Broadcast - You are partially protected if you were live on-air, took all reasonable precautions to ensure a libel didn't happen, had no reason to suspect it would and had no effective control over the speaker.

The Defamation Act 2013

The Defamation Act 2013 aims to ensure that a fair balance is struck between the right to freedom of expression and the protection of someone's reputation.

There are a number of important changes to the law of defamation:

- A requirement for claimants to show that they have suffered serious harm or substantial loss before suing for libel (in the same way as has always existed for slander).
- Introducing new statutory defences of Truth and Honest Opinion to replace the defences of Justification and Fair Comment.
- Introducing a defence of "responsible publication on matters of public interest" to protect investigative journalism.
- Increased protection for website operators that host user-generated content, providing they comply with a "take down" procedure to enable the complainant to resolve disputes directly with the author.
- Limits on those not resident in the UK taking action – so-called 'libel tourism'.

The Act only applies in England and Wales and not in Scotland or Northern Ireland.

The Katie Hopkins Case

The "serious harm or substantial loss" test was originally thought to apply only if someone had lost their job or money as a result of being defamed.

However, in 2017, food writer and blogger Jack Monroe took libel action against newspaper columnist and broadcaster Katie Hopkins for inferring in a tweet that she was involved in or supported the desecration of war memorials.

Awarding damages of £24,000 against Ms Hopkins, Mr Justice Warby said her words had caused Ms Monroe "serious harm to her reputation" and "real and substantial distress". Ms Hopkins also had to pay costs running into six figures.

Experts say as a result of this judgment, courts will allow robust debate online but if comments cause serious reputational harm, legal action will be upheld.

Differences in Scotland

There are some significant differences in defamation law in Scotland.

In England and Wales, people have one year to make a claim for defamation. In Scotland, people have three years.

Some of the language used in the Scottish legal system is different:

- The claimant in a defamation case in Scotland is called a "pursuer"
- The defendant in a defamation case in Scotland is called a "defender"
- The defence that a statement is true is called "veritas"
- Evidence heard is called a "proof"
- There is a defence of "Fair Comment" which is similar to Honest Opinion

Differences in Northern Ireland

The Defamation Act 2013 does not apply in Northern Ireland. This means that libel law in the province remains the same as that which existed in England and Wales prior to that date.

The threshold of serious harm or substantial loss doesn't apply and therefore a libel action still very much relies on damage to someone's reputation.

Appendix
The McAlpine Case

This is the most important and high-profile Twitter Libel case in the UK to date and vividly illustrates what can happen legally when gossip on Twitter goes too far. It also shows the vulnerability of people tweeting and retweeting serious allegations.

Lord McAlpine, the former Conservative party treasurer, took legal action for libel against broadcasters and individual tweeters in 2012.

Background

The BBC's current affairs TV programme Newsnight broadcast a report on child abuse in a North Wales care home.

The source of the story, former care home resident Steve Messham, claimed he had been raped and sexually abused by a "leading Tory politician of the Thatcher era".

Lord McAlpine was not named by the BBC – but the programme led to a speculation on Twitter with him being wrongly accused of being a sex abuser. This is known as 'jigsaw identification' where small bits of information are given out and pieced together.

Mr Messham later withdrew his claims of being abused by the politician, saying it had been a case of mistaken identity.

A few days after the Newsnight report, the ITV programme This Morning featured a live interview with the Prime Minister.

Presenter Philip Schofield handed a bemused-looking David Cameron a list of names of alleged paedophiles he said he had found on the internet.

It emerged that some of the names – including Lord McAlpine's - could briefly be seen by viewers due to the camera angle.

Lord McAlpine's Reaction

Lord McAlpine said he had been in a state of "horrendous shock" after hearing the allegations that he was linked to child abuse.

Speaking on BBC Radio 4, he said nothing was as bad as being accused of being a paedophile.

He went on: "They are quite rightly figures of public hatred – and suddenly to find yourself a figure of public hatred, unjustifiably, is terrifying."

In the interview, Lord McAlpine said the accusation "gets into your bones, it makes you angry, and that's extremely bad for you to be angry, and it gets into your soul and you just think there is something wrong with the world."

The peer was asked about London Mayor Boris Johnson's comment that to call someone a paedophile was to "consign them to the lowest circle of hell while they're still alive".

Lord McAlpine said: "Absolutely. I think it pretty much describes what happened to me".

Lord McAlpine's solicitor, Andrew Reid, said the peer and his family had been caused "immeasurable distress which cannot be rectified."

Consequences for the Broadcasters

An allegation of paedophilia is one of the most serious slurs damaging to someone's reputation and consequently, it commands libel damages at the very top of the scale.

Lord McAlpine took libel action against both the BBC and ITV. Both claims were swiftly settled at the High Court in London.

Keep It Legal

The BBC paid £185,000 damages and ITV paid £125,000 along with substantial legal costs.

Unreserved apologies were made by both parties for the damage and distress caused.

At the BBC, the erroneous Newsnight report later partly led to the resignation of the Director General, George Entwistle.

At ITV, management took "appropriate disciplinary action" against Philip Schofield and some of the This Morning production staff.

Consequences for Tweeters

The law concerning Twitter is clear. If you defame someone, you can be sued for libel. Until the McAlpine case, nobody had seriously attempted to exercise that right.

Lord McAlpine's solicitor, Andrew Reid, engaged specialists to trace all mentions of Lord McAlpine on Twitter and other social media.

All messages are preserved on Twitter's computer servers even if they are not publicly viewable or have been deleted.

After realising they could be sued, Mr Reid said about 1,000 tweeters had written to Lord McAlpine to apologise for falsely linking him to the child abuse allegations.

They were all sent a letter saying that Lord McAlpine did not intend to create any hardship but he would be requesting a small donation to the BBC's Children In Need charity.

The accompanying 'Twitter Reconciliation Form' asked for home address, occupation, the number of Twitter followers, whether the offending tweet was original or a retweet, whether the tweet was deleted and, in the case of re-tweets, the source of the original.

It was decided that people with less than 500 followers would not be pursued if they made a £25 donation to Children In Need in lieu of damages.

<u>Sally Bercow</u>

Around the time of the Newsnight broadcast, the outspoken wife of the House of Commons Speaker, Sally Bercow, tweeted her 57,000 followers:-

"Why is Lord McAlpine trending? *innocent face*"

Lord McAlpine's lawyers issued and served proceedings for libel against Mrs Bercow, claiming damages of £50,000 and an apology.

Mrs Bercow defended her tweet saying it was not libellous and arguing it was merely mischievous.

In the High Court, Mrs Bercow's QC, William McCormick, argued that the phrase "innocent face" was merely an indication that the tweet should be read in a deadpan manner.

But Lord McAlpine's barrister, Sir Edward Garnier QC, said only a "moron in a hurry" would have been unfamiliar with the context in which the words were tweeted.

The High Court ruled that the tweet was defamatory and Mrs Bercow agreed to make an undisclosed financial settlement to a charity of Lord McAlpine's choice.

In his judgment, Britain's most senior libel judge, Mr Justice Tugendhat, dismissed Mrs Bercow's argument that the question she had posed in the tweet was entirely neutral.

He reasoned that many of her followers shared an interest in current affairs and would have been up-to-date with the Newsnight story.

He ruled that her inclusion of the words "innocent face" revealed the question was "insincere and ironical".

Keep It Legal

It was, therefore, reasonable to infer that she meant Lord McAlpine was trending because he fitted the description of the unnamed abuser.

After the ruling, Mrs Bercow said she had learned her lesson the hard way and saying the ruling should be seen as a warning to all social media users.

She said comments could sometimes be "held to be seriously defamatory, even when you do not intend them to be defamatory and do not make any express accusation."

Alan Davies

A number of other prominent people with large Twitter followings have also apologised to Lord McAlpine.

Alan Davies is a comedian and panellist on BBC2's QI programme. He has almost 450,000 Twitter followers.

He tweeted: "Any clues as to who the Tory paedophile is?" He subsequently retweeted a response naming Lord McAlpine.

Mr Davies' lawyers said he didn't intend to retweet the message and he apologised.

He paid £15,000 in damages, which Lord McAlpine donated to the Royal Chelsea Hospital, and made a contribution to costs.

Lord McAlpine's lawyer, Andrew Reid, said the comedian's "reckless retweet" of a defamatory statement "fanned the work of internet trolls".

George Monbiot

Writer and newspaper columnist George Monbiot, who has 58,000 followers, wrote to Lord McAlpine saying, "I'm feeling worse about this than anything else I have ever done – though I realise it is nothing by comparison to what you have gone through with the help of my stupidity and thoughtlessness."

He went on: "I helped to stoke an atmosphere of innuendo around an innocent man."

Mr Monbiot reached an unprecedented settlement with Lord McAlpine where he pledged to carry out three years of work for three charities amounting to £25,000.

Of the settlement, he said it reflected well on Lord McAlpine "who is seeking nothing for himself but wants to see work done which could be of great benefit to others".

Mr Monbiot had a cautionary word for Twitter users: "Please make sure you check your facts and think before you tweet."

Lessons Learned

Anyone who uses Twitter must recognise they are not taking part in a private conversation among their friends in a pub or café but that their tweets are 'broadcasts' and 'published'.

This includes repeating the words of others in a retweet. Not only can your tweets be read by your own followers but can be retweeted by them and read by many others around the world.

Tweets cannot be deleted and remain on Twitter's servers. This means they can be retrieved by specialists working for lawyers who suspect libel.

Twitter has given everyone in the world instant access to a public forum. Until recently, most people were constrained from comment by the traditional gatekeepers – journalists, broadcasters and publishers.

Sadly, Lord McAlpine died on 17th January 2014 aged 71 at his home in Italy.

Part 2
Contempt of Court
The Right to a Fair Trial

What Is Contempt of Court?

Contempt of Court is the law that protects the judicial process. It is separate to Defamation but equally as important.

It is wide-ranging and covers things from people's behaviour in the court itself, ensuring court orders are obeyed and making sure nothing is published or broadcast which might cause legal proceedings to go wrong.

Ensuring a Fair Trial

One of the most important parts of the Contempt of Court law is about protecting people's right to a fair trial.

You become guilty of Contempt when you broadcast or publish material that creates a SUBSTANTIAL RISK of SERIOUS PREJUDICE to active legal proceedings such as an ongoing court case, regardless of your intent.

When Do Legal Proceedings Become Active?

Legal proceedings become active at the point of someone's ARREST not charge.

Someone does NOT have to be charged with an offence for the matter to become legally active. From the moment someone is arrested, you have to be careful what you say.

What Are The Dangers of Contempt?

Contempt can happen if a radio presenter, guest, caller or social media user passes their own judgment on a pending or current court case or broadcasts or tweets information which may prejudice jurors – like revealing a defendant's previous convictions for example.

The opinion of a radio presenter, a podcaster or tweeter (based on what he/she may have read in the paper, seen on TV or heard in news bulletins) could easily colour the view of a juror and/or allow the defendant to claim that he/she will be unable to receive a fair trial and therefore could walk free.

Many people discuss ongoing trials in the pub or in conversation – but it's vital to understand that you cannot broadcast or discuss ongoing legal proceedings on radio or on social media in the same way.

Consequences of Committing Contempt

Unlike libel which is a CIVIL matter and settled with the award of damages and apologies, contempt of court is a CRIMINAL matter.

This means it carries serious penalties and punishments. You could actually be imprisoned for something you say on the radio or podcast or tweet or post.

If you commit contempt, a judge can issue a summons for you to appear in court and you can be arrested.

A contempt case is usually only closed once you have "purged your contempt" by sincerely apologised in open court before a judge.

The best advice here is – NEVER EVER discuss or comment on an ongoing trial or pending court case.

You should also ensure you don't comment on someone after they've been arrested or a warrant has been issued for their arrest.

And the consequences of committing contempt don't just end with you. There are much bigger considerations.

For example, your broadcast, tweets and posts could prejudice a trial and lead to a guilty person walking free. Or a re-trial might have to be arranged at a potential cost of thousands of pounds.

Unguarded words could put the life of a protected witness in danger or cause serious psychological damage to the victim of sexual assault.

Court reporting is a specialized journalistic skill and should be left to the professionals.

Two Examples of Contempt on Radio

Rock FM

Two presenters at Rock FM in Preston, Mark Kaye and Jude Vause, were arrested and taken to court for something they said during the multiple murder trial of Dr Harold Shipman in 2000.

The trial had been going on a long time. During the station's afternoon drive-time show, Mark said the following, with Jude in the background joining in:

Mark: "I'm supposed to be delicate but I really don't care. Harold Shipman's trial is going into its umpteenth month…"

Jude: "Guilty, guilty…"

Mark: "…It's innocent until proved guilty as sin. Put us taxpayers out of our misery because we're paying for this. Admit to it. It's a fair cop. You're caught red-handed. Be done with it"

The incident was considered particularly serious because jurors might have heard what the presenters said on their way home from the trial (which was taking place at nearby Preston Crown Court), thus potentially prejudicing the case.

It could have led to the abandonment of the trial costing taxpayers hundreds of thousands of pounds.

Trial judge Mr Justice Forbes described what had happened as "just about as irresponsible a piece of broadcasting as I've ever heard."

Luckily none of the jurors had heard the broadcast. Rock FM's boss, Michelle Surrell, had to "purge contempt" by sincerely apologising to the court and the judge.

Shipman was convicted of 15 counts of murder and sentenced to 15 life sentences to run concurrently. He hanged himself in his cell in 2004.

Beacon FM

The breakfast team at Beacon FM, Mark Peters and Lisa Freame, were removed from their show when they opened the phone lines to discuss the trial of Ian Huntley in 2003. Huntley was convicted of killing two little girls in the village of Soham, Cambridgeshire.

To make matters worse, the presenters even aired their own theories about what happened and expressed their opinions on the case which was ongoing at the time. During the reporting of Huntley's evidence, they said on-air:

Mark – "It's almost like the most unbelievably made up story in the world ever, really isn't it? Well, I personally think it is. I can't believe that any member of the jury is going to believe that story."

Lisa – "The trouble is we don't know enough facts and we've had loads of messages in saying it may have been an accident for one of the girls but does he really expect us all to believe it was an accident for the other…. And they're saying if it was an accident, then he'd be showing some signs of remorse."

Although they lost their jobs, neither they or the radio station were prosecuted for contempt because the trial was taking place at the Old

Bailey in London, well away from their broadcast area of Telford in Shropshire.

This means what they said was unlikely to have prejudiced the jury because they would have been unable to hear it.

Of course, these days that would not apply as almost every radio station is streamed online via websites and apps and available to hear anywhere in the world.

The Danger of Breaking Court Orders

Although commenting on a case is one way you can commit contempt, there are various other ways:

- Naming the victim of a sexual assault or rape
- Revealing previous convictions before the end of a trial
- Identifying child witnesses
- Naming blackmail victims
- Publicising details of people under witness protection

Usually all these things are covered by court orders which must not be breached.

Everyone is a reporter these days. Some journalists and lawyers are worried that Tweeters, Facebookers and bloggers will fail to understand the impact of breaking court orders.

The media is automatically banned from naming the victims of sexual assaults who have life-long anonymity. The same rules apply to social media.

Two Examples of Contempt on Social Media

Ched Evans

The Welsh footballer Ched Evans was convicted of raping a 19-year-old woman in 2012.

The case generated more than 6,000 tweets with some people deciding to name the victim suggesting she was "crying rape" and "money grabbing".

Seven men and two women were fined by magistrates for breaking the law. They pleaded guilty and said they didn't realise they had broken the law by naming her - but ignorance is no defence.

James Bulger

Two men who put photos on Twitter and Facebook said to show the killers of James Bulger received nine-month jail sentences, suspended for 15 months, for being in contempt of court.

Neil Harkins, 35, and Dean Liddle, 28, admitted posting pictures purporting to depict the killers as adults, two days after the 20th anniversary of the murder.

Jon Venables and Robert Thompson were jailed for life for murdering the two-year-old in Merseyside in 1993. They were released in 2001 and given new identities.

A High Court order prohibits the publication of any images or information claiming to identify or locate the pair, even if it's not actually them. The global ban also covers material published on the internet.

After being contacted by officials, Harkins took the post down and apologised but it had already been shared by 24,000 people. Liddle later said he hadn't realised how serious the situation was.

More Things to Avoid Saying or Doing

- Revealing a previous conviction (or convictions)
- Saying someone has confessed or admitted the crime when they haven't
- Accusing somebody of a more serious crime
- Revealing prosecution evidence before the trial gets underway
- Making derogatory comments suggesting a motive
- Commenting about someone's character related to the issue at the trial
- Saying whether you believe they are innocent or guilty
- Seeking or revealing jury deliberations

Attorney General Inquiry

The Attorney General, Jeremy Wright QC MP, launched an inquiry in late 2017 to examine if the court system is being undermined by social media and whether Contempt of Court laws need to change to cope with the modern world.

He said the problem was that if a social media post goes viral, it can be seen by thousands of people including jurors and that could prejudice a fair trial.

Mr Wright explained: "Members of the public who don't understand what the Contempt of Court Act says probably don't realise what damage their piece of social media commentary or comment might do."

The trial of two girls aged 13 and 14 accused of murdering Angela Wrightson in Hartlepool had to be discontinued because of a torrent of social media outrage and vile abuse against the defendants that threatened to prejudice the hearing. The girls were subsequently convicted in a second trial.

The AG is asking lawyers and judges to cite cases when social media had interfered with a trial and recommend any changes as a result of their experiences to protect against "trial by social media".

Keep It Legal

Why Do Newspapers 'Get Away with' Contempt?

Many broadcasters question why some tabloid newspapers avoid prosecution for obviously ignoring the law by publishing details after someone has been arrested.

Newspapers rely on an argument known as the 'fade factor' - the gap between publication and trial which can often be up to 10 months.

They argue that the longer the gap, the less the "substantial risk of serious prejudice" of the jury.

But this is risky. Newspapers are able to flaunt the contempt laws because they act collectively, have good lawyers and lots of financial resources to fund any legal fights. It is not something you should do as a broadcaster, podcaster or tweeter.

The Christopher Jefferies Case

When someone is arrested and subsequently released after questioning without charge, newspapers can find themselves at risk of libel action as well as for Contempt of Court.

Christopher Jefferies, a 65-year-old retired schoolteacher, was arrested after the murder in Bristol of one of his tenants, landscape architect Jo Yeates, 25, in 2010.

Immediately after his arrest and because of the way he looked, tabloid newspapers described him variously as "strange", "weird", "lewd", "creepy", a stalker, a peeping tom and linked him to previous paedophile and murder cases.

The headline in the Mirror was "Jo Suspect Is Peeping Tom" and in The Sun, "The Strange Mr Jefferies".

He was released after questioning and never charged. Another man, Vincent Tabak, was subsequently convicted of Jo's murder and jailed.

Not only did Mr Jefferies accept substantial libel damages (totalling approximately £600,000) and apologies from eight newspapers but two papers were also successfully prosecuted by the Attorney General for Contempt of Court. The Mirror had to pay £50,000 and The Sun £18,000.

Giving evidence to the Leveson Inquiry into Press Ethics in 2011, Mr Jefferies said: "In the coverage of my case, there was flagrant lawlessness. The smears were so extensive that it's true to say there will always be people who don't know me who will retain the impression that I'm some kind of very weird character indeed who is best avoided."

In 2014, ITV made an excellent two-part drama about the case called The Lost Honour of Christopher Jefferies. Actor Jason Watkins won a BAFTA award for his portrayal of Mr Jefferies.

The Internet and Juries

If you're selected to be on a jury at a trial, the judge will warn you against researching the history and background online as well as tweeting, posting and blogging about the case.

This is because juries are meant to make up their mind only from the evidence that is presented in court and not be influenced by other things.

Research shows that jurors are going to the internet to look for background to cases.

It may be that the principle of the sanctity of the jury room cannot be maintained in the face of modern communications and social media.

Of course, jury members have always been able to go to a library to look things up or be influenced by friends and gossip with neighbours. It's just that the internet and social media make it simpler and easier.

Keep It Legal

It's important that the integrity of the jury system should be preserved and protected.

When you serve on a jury, you take an oath. When you disobey that oath or when you disobey the orders of a judge – and you're found out – you are likely to be held in contempt of court.

The Lord Chief Justice says a custodial sentence for a juror doing this is "virtually inevitable"

In 2015 a new criminal offence of juror misconduct was created to catch jurors who researched details about a case including information about a judge, witnesses or defendant.

Tweeting from Court

Video and audio recording has long been barred from courts. In general, that applies to tweeting and texting too.

Members of the public are NOT allowed to tweet or text from court without permission.

The former Lord Chief Justice, Lord Judge, says the danger of tweeting is likely to be most acute during criminal trials.

"Witnesses who are out-of-court may be informed of what has already happened in court and so coached or briefed before they then give evidence," he said.

In addition, ordinary people in the public gallery could hear information that the jury may have been prevented from hearing, for example the identity of a rape victim. But this cannot be reported.

Therefore, the danger of a trial being seriously prejudiced or impeded is obvious.

However, the guidance says bona fide journalists ARE allowed to tweet without permission because they understand the rules and don't pose a danger of interference to the proper administration of justice.

Explaining why journalists should be treated differently from the public, Lord Judge said: "The difference is that John and Jane Citizen are less likely to understand the rules of contempt than most journalists who come into my court."

Differences in Scotland

In Scottish courts, there is a verdict of 'Not Proven' alongside Guilty and Not Guilty. This is an expression that there was insufficient evidence, for example, "The charge was found not proven". It is an acquittal, which is the same as Not Guilty where the accused walks free.

Scottish juries have 15 members not 12 as in England and Wales. There are no opening speeches in criminal trials. The jury makes a decision based on the evidence before hearing what the advocates say.

The prosecutor in Scotland is called the "Procurator Fiscal" and judge issue a "decree" rather than a judgment.

The best advice:

If in doubt, leave it out.

Part 3
Injunctions
The Right to Privacy

What Is an Injunction and a Super-Injunction?

An INJUNCTION is a court order which prevents the publication of certain details of a legal case including identities or actions.

Injunctions – sometimes known as 'gagging orders' - were originally created to protect people whose lives might be at risk if their details were made public, such as child sex offenders.

However, with the passing of the Human Rights Act 1998, judges began to extend the powers of injunctions. Entertainers, sports stars, actors and many more have used injunctions to protect their privacy.

A SUPER-INJUNCTION is a powerful legal order which not only prevents the media from reporting the details of a story covered by an injunction but also forbids mention of the very existence of the injunction itself.

Users ignoring injunctions or reporting the existence of super-injunctions could be found guilty of contempt of court and sued for invasion of privacy, while those making false accusations could be sued for libel.

How Does a Super-Injunction Work?

The best way to see how a super-injunction works is to examine a hypothetical example.

Keep It Legal

A Premiership football star asks the High Court to stop a Sunday newspaper publishing a kiss-and-tell story, saying he's a victim of blackmail by a girl he met at a party.

If a judge agrees to a super-injunction, the newspaper is not only stopped from reporting the allegations but is also prevented from saying that the footballer went to court to gag the paper.

If the newspaper breaks this super-injunction by reporting the existence of an injunction, the editor could be prosecuted for being in contempt of court.

It's said super-injunctions are very rarely granted and only for short periods.

More common is an ANONYMISED INJUNCTION where not only is something legally stopped but the names of either or both parties to the proceedings are not revealed.

Are Tweeters Waging War on Super-Injunctions?

Twitter has found itself at the centre of the debate about super-injunctions.

While newspapers, broadcasters and other traditional mainstream media are being restricted in what they can report, thousands of Twitter users have posted tweets and retweets circulating information covered by injunctions and super-injunctions.

Are these tweeters beyond the reach of the law?

In practice, legal experts expect tweeters to find safety in numbers if enough defy an injunction simultaneously.

It's not the letter of the law that protects tweeters, but the sheer difficulty of singling out and tracking down so many offenders.

Esteemed legal analyst and broadcaster Joshua Rozenberg says: "Clearly they are at risk, but if there are a lot of them there's little chance of them being prosecuted… although if there was one individual who could be seen to have instigated the whole thing, that would be very different."

The Ryan Giggs Case

Footballer Ryan Giggs obtained an injunction to prevent publication of details of an alleged affair with reality TV star Imogen Thomas.

Newspapers and broadcasters were initially unable to name Giggs or even refer to the existence of an injunction.

However, a tweeter revealed Giggs' identity. Public interest was such that the record for visits to Twitter was exceeded.

The allegations were repeatedly retweeted by 75,000 users making it difficult to prosecute any one individual.

The judge declined to renew Giggs' injunction. No action was taken against the tweeters.

Nevertheless, legal action was instigated by Giggs against Twitter in an attempt to obtain information on which tweeters were involved.

Paradoxically, this then led to the footballer's name and the allegations being repeated many more times across the internet and, as a consequence, by the mainstream media.

Remember:-
Tweet in haste,
Repent at leisure.

The best advice:-
If In Doubt, Leave It Out

About the Authors

PAUL CHANTLER has spent 35 years in the radio industry as a journalist, presenter, producer and programme executive. He was Group Programme Director at three of the UK's biggest radio groups in the 1990s and over the last 15 years has built a highly successful radio consultancy company with clients in the UK, Ireland, Europe and India. He is co-author of the textbook Essential Radio Journalism, originally published 25 years ago. He regularly conducts seminars for radio groups on media law and compliance.

www.paulchantler.com
chantler@aol.com
@PaulChantler

PAUL HOLLINS is an award-winning radio presenter, voice over artist and author. He started his career at Key 103 in Manchester before working at BRMB in Birmingham, Capital FM London and Heart 106.2 in London. In 1999 he set-up the radio content and syndication company Blue Revolution which is now one of Europe's leading providers of programming and radio services. Paul currently presents on Smooth Radio.

paul@bluerevolution.com
www.bluerevolution.com
@thePaulHollins

Printed in Great Britain
by Amazon